Masculine Happiness

For my Mother
Leonora

Masculine Happiness

David Foster-Morgan

Seren is the book imprint of
Poetry Wales Press Ltd.
57 Nolton Street, Bridgend, Wales, CF31 3AE
www.serenbooks.com
facebook.com/SerenBooks
twitter@SerenBooks

ISBN: 978-1-78172-267-1
ebook: 978-1-78172-274-9
Kindle: 978-1-78172-281-7

A CIP record for this title is available from the British Library.

The publisher acknowledges the financial assistance of the Welsh Books Council.

Cover Painting: 'Moon and Girl' © Meirion Ginsberg.
Photograph supplied by Martin Tinney Gallery.

Printed in Bembo by Bell & Bain Ltd, Glasgow.

Contents

F O'H

There are better reasons to read
Frank O'Hara than a drinker in a bar
lost in reading a beat-up old collection.

And if this were Bastille Day I'd celebrate
that one English lunatic the mob liberated
when they broke those terrible doors.

Train times, travelling to dinner parties –
remind me of Evelyn Waugh: escape,
familial society and bored hedonism;

but hamburgers and the sun open up
the canyons of New York: its yellow stones
embarrassed by their million eyeglasses.

The Anthology of American Poetry
has eight poems by F O'H, though not
the one that made the drinker walk.

I am reminded to read poets from Ghana,
recall their names; have more to say of
Verlaine than cafés and absinthe;

of Bonnard, to step scene by scene through
one of his afternoons, dissolve in light
– though I fear his work is sentimental;

and Genet, who could live in a prison,
however it was lit – it was Behan
had the reprieved man hang himself.

Gauloises or Picayunes – does it matter?
Their incense meandering like the shadow
on a winding seventy-eight –

the needle measuring back the anticipation
in a dim room, waiting for *Lady Day*
to step into the light.

Star-Spangled Banner

In the cathedral of the echo
The lock is picked with a DIN plug
Slotted in the amp's socket

America in the key of electricity
In the day's thirtieth hour
When the moon's split
And the sun *ain't* going to show
When the light is white light
Magnesium flare white
The light you see when you die
And you know it's *all the same fucking day*
On the road, on trains, on the telegraph wires
It's always been the same fucking day

America is alive in the telegraph wires
Crazy Horse is alive
Out in the desert he's multiplying
Fifty spots on his body
Fifty Crazy Horses on each spot
Turn the kaleidoscope
Fifty million Crazy Horses in the desert
They're plugged in
Flashing like neon signs
Flashing so you can see them from the moon
Flashing the Star-Spangled Banner
Flashing *Girls Girls Girls*
Flashing *Jesus Saves*
Flashing *We Never Close*

America is closed
I went into the desert yesterday
To talk with my brother
There was a fence made of electrified barbed wire
A painted sign said *Private Property*
I couldn't read the other side
I couldn't get to see my brother
And there was Crazy Horse
The original Crazy Horse
Wearing this beat-up army blanket
And I said *it was never meant to be like this*
And he said *there is always America*
Didn't you know America is in the wires
Tune in your radio
America is the Big Bang
America is the sound of imploding stars

Buenos Aires in 1936

with its three hours and two seasons of difference
suits this Borges.
I like to imagine their parallel lives:
those other men called Borges
who seek my correspondence.

Mr Gordie Borges of Glasgow
– a marine engineer on the Clyde –
writes of his travels.
The style is R. L. Stevenson's,
journeys imagined from the engine rooms
of moored ships;
but so salacious, a sure stimulus for one of my
Gaucho romances – not today.

And Dr Georges Borges writes
from the zoological museum of Paris.
A new specimen: skeleton of a gibbon,
head of a cat. The felo-simian a fraud,
but full of possibility,
surely it deserves a place
in the bestiary of my imagination.

I sleep badly and the third letter troubles me.
Dr Georg Borges of Berlin has written,
for so long my favourite correspondent.
His dealings in Arabic manuscripts
delighted my interest:
a new fragment of Heraclitus
or kabalistic formula; and his knack
of finding that most organic Arabic script
in the weave of cloth: once
the names – a whole progress of sultans –
in the binding of *one thousand and one nights*.

The Doctor has taken a dark turn.
He writes of the real monsters
they make in Germany today.
No longer do they look into forests
or at the bare country,
they find their goblins in the street
point to real men, order them as demons,
call them beasts.

Masculine Happiness

John Wayne is *warm, tired and had*
just the right number of drinks. Firelight
and the stars of Arizona surround his bed:
a saddle blanket rolled out in the desert night.

News headlines of a foreign war: the reporter's
hair and blue eyes match her checked scarf;
and a voice behind me starts: *who's having her,*
insulted when I won't laugh as he starts to laugh.

On another channel Bob Mitchum's an old sea captain:
safe on land while his son's submarine is overdue;
drinking cognac from a dark bottle, he finishes it all,
and floats into the sleep of drunk and drowned men.
Sick the next morning, his steps slow and unsure,
like a shipwrecked sailor exploring a new shore.

Cigar

Sometimes it is just a Cigar.
Freud knew the bourgeois pleasure
of the connoisseur.
The pucker of paper skin;
the pinch of smoke breathed in.
Like the lovers who smoothed
and teased, plucked the hairs
of his beard.

Out in the tobacco fog of history
Che Guevara sits cross-legged,
cigar butt tight between teeth
and cheek. He offers *Habanos*
and alternatives to the world's press.
Smoke bubbles from his
great dyspepsia of revolution.
The cloud thickens, his pointing
nicotine-stained hands
the last to fade.

John reaches his hands into the fog;
under the Tantalus heat
Helga holds half-an-inch from his skin.
The salt shock, the burn
happens higher: *where it won't show.*
Helga – real name Kylie –
likes a cigar now
more heady than coffee
and the taste is mild.

At the Guggenheim in Bilbao, a show of...

i.r. *Cai Guo-Qiang*

:: An exhibition hall filled with broken... :: Iron plates like scales left by... :: Gunpowder-burns on paper wind like... :: Early firearms in the shape of... :: Men's skin tattooed with... :: Wounds like white new hatched... :: Improvised weapons with the breath of... :: All jewels are the eggs of... :: Buckled train carriages like fanning... :: The fifth mysterious invention was the... :: A Buddhist philosophy guarded by... :: A Taoist cosmology revealed by... :: A Maoist rhetoric that ignores... :: The phoenix's opposites are... :: Shy lizards are the real... :: Fragments from an epic fantasy of... :: A virgin threatened by... :: A festival of drums and dancing... :: Comic verses staring... :: A child's heroes may be... :: A bride's dress embroidered with... :: A drunk sees pink... :: A spicy soup named after... :: Porcelain decorated with... :: Tethered kites with heads of... :: Museum attendants with faces like... :: A concept realised in placing... :: A floodlight show throws shadow... :: A gallery coiled like sleeping... :: The mist summoned by... :: The Olympic Games opened by... :: Pyrotechnics fall like mating... :: A world that will end in the mouths of...

Turning

it's something a child would do   like staring into the sun or
    eating the thing that makes you sick   you lift one foot
        put it down T-shaped   with your other foot
            you bring it round

T-step and around   round and you go around
    the colours change   you do feel sick
        something a child would do

T-step and round   half a minute to adapt
    your feet   light above the ground
        your breath steadies
            then slows down

slows, and you watch the world go round
waving coral cyan umber azure   lapis and vermilion pure
    the walls are white
        and someone's   top is poppy red

weightless   a child spun round   your breath keeps going
    legs turning   T-step and round
        eventually you do slow down

your legs stumble the circle falters   your breathing   pauses
    gets shorter   down to a steady turn
        nauseous on your return   coral cyan umber pure

steady turn to unsteady stop   a child
    where the walls are white
        and Linda wears a poppy top

Annunciation

Each night I come to Nazareth
and to your green, rocky shore.

You wait like the calm sea
waits for dawn.

Night rooms brood
on the shocked corporal:

how the body's curves
broaden,

and how flesh knots
against its stigma.

The night is crowded
...so many voices.

Come away
my words are for you alone.

The Stones at Whithorn Priory

The earliest is not entirely a cross,
more a Greek letter, faint amongst Latin,
a circle quartered horizontal and vertical,
its four points, a frame for carving a man.

The Golgotha stone is closest,
three empty crucifixes overlap in relief,
like big-sleeved angels ready to fly,
worn as tools from a craftsman's hands.

Their sculptors knew the charisma of circles,
the open smile of a healing teacher,
the chipped sockets of a flotsam skull,
or bright seals' eyes flashing on the swell.

In the museum the stones stand in a ring,
arranged for resemblance and chronology,
in this correct light they are hazy,
faces from a haar, or fever.

Entering The Warhol Chapel

You'd probably walk past the first time,
check the house numbers either side
before you decided on this door.
One of those not-so-old churches
built into the terrace, so it's hard to see
where it ends and the houses begin.

In the porch your entry is replayed
on half-a-dozen black-and-white screens:
the door opening, a semicircle of light
spreading over the tiles, you hesitate,
try the handle, open the door
just wide enough and, closing it gently,
find yourself on television,
in a room lit by your own image
replayed for as long as you watch.

There is a bed on the screen:
next to the door, high, a large single
or small double, made up with blankets,
a figure printed on its bedspread.
If you turn around you'll be able to touch
its waffled texture, see Elvis: the young
gunslinger in the film *Flaming Star.*

Sometimes *The King* can be heard
singing from inside: *Love Me Tender*
and *Jailhouse Rock* are available
from a jukebox inside the transept
if you have an old penny.

Hound Dogs

Noon and Ian's killed his quota, a five-year-old
brown bear under cover in the truck. He stops at mount
Guitar-on, ready drench in its waterfalls.

Hot with capability, hungry for more Nature.

The scent of sweet apricot drifts through the pines.
His dogs slink off; follow their noses into the wood.
In the water there is a young woman swimming.

He tracks her, gives one of his *high-testosterone hellos*.

Unfazed, she swims up close, stands naked
and looks straight at him. *You are an arty-miss.*
She smiles, wry, and fingers her gold name pendant.

His hounds jump in, nuzzling between them.

Artemis shudders her offence, pushes-off splashing.
Unbalanced, Ian falls, struggles onto the bank
calls to his dogs: *Roy-boy, Elvis come here, help me.*

The hounds look at him.

They lurch; he finds his flit-stag nature, fleet
through the trees, but Roy-boy catches him in
a leg hold, slipped with a subtle turn of his body.

Ian hardly feels Elvis' mouth on his neck.

Tryst

Everything in the room is white or plain wood.
The square bed has been stripped of its cover
and pulled out from the wall. Geri in the centre,
hums *Don't Let Me Be Misunderstood*
and folds her legs in half-lotus position.
Tom walks slowly, circles the bed, sits
behind her. His thighs touch her hips,
he massages her neck with a hard palm motion,
she un-crosses her legs, pulls herself forward,
he puts two fingers into her anus, lifts
himself on his knees. She straightens, tips
him over, pins him down, and bites hard
on his ear. Tom flinches, orgasms.
Geri lets go, pokes out her bloody Tongue.

Strigil

It aches on the way back from stone to supple.
Steam heat, dry heat clothe his friend with sweat,
adrift between tropics neither can settle,
hot blood or bronze. The cold most secret,
its half-forgotten, long-deferred caress,
scrapes a back bent carrying the world.
Exquisite twist of muscle, deep press,
make skin stretch, ease, give up its dirt.
Unflinching if the body should transgress
the classic line, its blunted point
gauges fat and age, wounds softness:
unflinching affection, unflinching hurt.
Outside attendants fold linen to dress
the deep blush, memory of its raw kiss.

The City Legend

Slowly the chimneys form against the sky,
like so many dirty glasses left overnight:

by the bedside, on bookshelves, the wardrobe,
something is familiar, in which room,

which road? Until the sun is found squinting
like an inch of beer at the end of the street.

In the biggest bed sitter in the world
and the biggest pisspot and shithouse too;

the pigeons peck discarded kebab boxes
and raindrops hang on plastic curtains around

The Roath Park pub, a scaffolding tent of night air,
smelling like an old tramp's snatch.

A door, sunk between shop fronts, opens half way
and a figure steps round, turns on one foot,

locks it and is off through the shadows. Going,
as you went, *to the hard work starting early,*

the first of the daylight ghosts on his way.
Your words, so many, still accompany me.

The yards he'll dig and hods he'll lift
before the van drops him back with a beep.

His sun will rise in a beer glass,
the sweet head forming; bitter body clearing.

Would you meet his eye over your *Echo,*
caught in a mirror or through the silt of drink;

and tell him of your day fitting ships, to you
the Millennium Stadium, the St David's Hotel,

were always great liners on our horizon.
And if he was patient or drunk enough

would you bother to get to the part
where one night the ships go back to sea;

or distracted by some *eleventh-hour tragedy,*
lonely in company across the bar:

throw yourself beneath tragedy's feet.
Play the lost puppy, sponge on her pity.

Now the sun has risen on City Road,
last night's remaining stragglers are dirty,

sinewy, and their big eyes so angry.
One picks up an abandoned lager can

takes a short drink and chucks it, crying over
his bloody drink and bloody money.

A drinker discovering in which room,
which street, the sun has found him.

Baboon

What remains is given up to burn.
Dressed in a smock, a tag on her toe.
Old, his mother rested on silk pillows,
calm voyager in the crematorium.
The family, kind-familiar words, stand
and sit in turn; Elgar's cello aches for thunder;
and afterwards a small container,
stone, heavy and cold in his hand.
Outside a petrol-hot afternoon.
His wife's black suit shines, hair teases the nape
of her neck. He phones, balances the urn in a box,
traffic is slotted, jammed back, the car is late;
and their three-year-old on top
of a van roof, screams: *I want to go home.*

Local Variety

They travel to see her tend strange nature.
Stopping where the earth turns gritty with blue coal,
going carefully over the angled slopes:
where the land falls and wild horses falter.
Square with muscle and thin-skinned, she keeps
the quiet of bird-less air. No fence encloses
her poppies, blue-red, like day-old bruises;
or pale tulips, varnished, like bloodless lips.
In her dreams she follows the water's course:
bubbling through hollow strata, past her mother,
silent like herself, and the breathing,
the last breathing of exhausted horses.
Back home, impressed, they talk and try
to put her odd colours under their same sky.

Who's living in the hanged man's house

Who's been cooking dead cat for his tea,
behind the cracked windows black with soot?

We can see the smoke rise from the end of the lane,
out through the gaps in the cocked chimney pot.

You, it's your dad, he's dumped the new tart
and come back to the village to live.

No, it's your big sister, the zombie,
she was here by the fire all of last night.

No, it's the ghost of that smelly old man,
who swung for three days before he was found.

The City Said No

As far as Victoria it was all planned
then she was going to use her new intuition.
Heading under the twilight to St Stephen's Hospital
going to see the *boy who almost died*.
Judy's city was expanding at each corner
from the bidding traffic of Trafalgar Square
through the Egyptian terraces of Belgravia
keeping in knowing parallel with the river,
until a turn and its dull water did not agree.
The river bodily contradicted her. She re-thought,
re-tried, but it argued, insisted, lay there, was right,
bickering long past visiting hours and miles downstream.
Another day it all seemed so ridiculous
talking brightly with the boy about motorcycles.

Butterfly

As Sally drinks, she slips further
and further out of the conversation.

A chrysalis of party clothes
propped back on the sofa.

Compassion and love for the world
are wings, bound tight inside her.

Sitting forward, she folds, eyes full
and tells: *how the world is so, so terrible*;

but people, so, so wonderful.
Her range is huge: wars of race and religion;

how she would choose the other side;
because, she too is guilty:

of a terrible bloody history.
Her gestures straining to hug *it all.*

As the drink weighs, Sally sinks back
comfortable in the chair; eyes closed

snuggling into her cocoon
she dreams of release:

a butterfly unfolding for the first time,
showing her wings to the world.

Land in Water

Sunrise is the settlement: hedges, shoals of sea
and beach lip: the parishes of Criccieth.
A house chimney foams smoke:
first life-sign in this half-dammed ground.
Sunk in the road there is no sight of coast
just surf sound and puddles salted by the earth.

Coming here, it was at Trawsfynydd,
the land became land-in-water.
In the thorn ring of mountains,
burnt in the world's forge,
the power station a block fort,
built to hold raiders' land.

Out from the dip I see a hill, mercury,
tall as the horizon. It is the sea.

Rip

A ripple, a girl, a woman, a wave,
from summertime coast to a winter at sea:
seven hundred strokes freestyle fighting the tide,
three hundred breaststrokes riding back to the shore.

Seven hundred breaths and the land's sunk away,
Elizabeth turning on the crest of a wave:
a pearl in a shell reflecting the sky,
a girl or a boat heading through spray.

*Float with the rip current
when you can't see the shore.*

★

A ripple, a girl, a wave, a woman,
Elizabeth basking, the sun closing her eyes,
she arches and floats as the big waves come in,
rolling back with them onto the beach.

Three girls hidden, nested in the dunes:
the eldest, the cleverest, the littlest of all,
wreathing and giggling in a hole in the sand;
they scatter like gulls when they are found.

*The rip current won't leave you
until you're far out to sea.*

★

A ripple, a wave, a woman, a girl,
calling *Abbey, Elisa, Beth* and *Mummy.*
Three girls watching from high sand dunes,
running off squealing when Elizabeth comes near.

Ten or twenty summers of games on the sand:
talk of boyfriends and husbands away inland;
four women, their arms crossed in a wheel,
make a bed to rock a baby to sleep.

You will not remember
the way back to the beach.

★

A wave, a girl, a ripple, a woman,
ten or twenty summers spent on the sand:
going strongly, going gently, into the sea;
coming slow, coming quick, back to the shore.

Twenty years and the land's sunk away,
Elizabeth turning on the crest of a wave:
a woman or girl heading through spray,
twenty years or an hour spent in the sea.

The tide, the gulls, the splash of the surf,
will all guide you back to the land.

November Level

There is muscle in this landscape
Under white-myopic light eyes don't look up

Rowan branches bow, touch the ground
Flash pagan signs in puddles filled with gold

My skin is thin metal
Warm blood is not enough

I put my hands together
Breathe the fever in their cup

Slumped between two summers
Remembered and to come

A shadow-rag on two suns
One set, one at dawn

What is all the cold of winter
But not air, not earth, not stone

No puzzle to the sun
The slow thickens

Winter is metal or fire
The quick quickens

An iron wall wears a shirt of light
Thin it flickers

Summer's yellow has downed
Air blushes in rose

The world is sheen
Colour raised from lead cold

Meeting My Eagle

Polar magnets, our feel for each other is
strongest at the point of turning away.
I stand in the doorway, you sit inside,
switch channels on the television.

There is a metal taste in my mouth,
the chew of tight cheeks, the texture
lifting me to the high balcony of a dream.
Looking over desert hills, into white sky.

I remember an eagle gliding into land,
perched behind me, shared my view.
The breeze in his feathers and my fine hair.
Afraid of the snap in his nature, I tensed.

He tasted my threat and thought of fight and
attacked: putting in his beak and claws.
We writhed, two branches on a sprung wind.
I saw into his eyes, he meant to blind me.

I am an animal ten times his size – broke him,
plucked him, snapped his chicken bones,
leaving him downy, four stumped:
poor ape, with only memories of flight.

I am awake now, so my eagle stays inside,
contained within the bone house of my skull.
Quiet, except our tension makes him stir,
all our confusion of metal and air.

I feel his head, it butts behind my nose.
In the hallway mirror I see his eyes:
spoked-copper wheels, stilled in amber,
holding the room, despite his ruined form.

Leo

In the thin night of August, a lion:
six stars looped, a resting tail and body;
three stars hooked, his neck and watching head.

A birch reaches, spear-flexed and balances
holding its shadow slack against its side,
silver and alone in the diluted sky.

We burn, still blushing with a hot day's sun,
cold and painted in strange colours,
violet and bronze, inside night's ribs.

Leo was my canopy, summer plush my bed,
a giggling one-year-old in sixty-nine,
kicking air on the lawn, all sound roared.

The Sausage Factory

The town in this poem is a town you know, the one famous for sausages. If you don't know a town famous for sausages then the town is your hometown. Either way, town or city, this poem is set three years ago from today.

At first people in the town were pleased when the sausage factory closed: left high and dry on the right side of town; once lorries thundered and hummed bringing in refrigerated pork; thundered and whined as they trucked the packed sausages out. If your town was the famous sausage town, a generation ago you would have spent a summer: boring hours with impossible machines, and one blessed afternoon when everyone gave in and pelted each other with pig guts, until you cried red tears from laughing, the fat soapy between your fingers and toes; for days afterwards you found dry gristle: behind your ears, in the seams of your clothing, between the folds, crevices in your skin. The factory that you are thinking of is closed, levelled, and they are digging new foundations. They are being very careful in sausage town. They have found human remains under the sausage factory, they admit to causing a little accidental cannibalism, but are keeping it in perspective, it is only one body and a few fingers and toes mixed in with the pig bones; and 80, 90, 125 years ago meatpacking was a difficult business. They prefer to talk about the dead man and an old scandal, from the time of your last major war, when the sausages poisoned people. There was a suspect with a foreign name, or who would look foreign to you, or who put poison in the sausages. It was always thought he ran away. So in your town or the other town, they are being careful with the human remains. The way they would be careful with one of the three million bodies buried near the Great Wall of China, or the blasted remains of a navigator found near the Great Western Railway; or a corpse found near a wall or railway line in your town.

Two men

have told me the meaning of life:
one a lecturer in Metaphysics, the second
a burnt-out case.

The case walked into the university
asked to see the Professor of Philosophy.
While he waited he told me the meaning
was two bus rides away, under a bridge,
he had diagrams that would help. Though
I didn't study his many pentangles,
the college porters insisted he keep
them as they walked him out.
This happened every year
or two: a new thinker
his influences
chemical.

The lecturer's logic followed Aristotle.
He told me how he woke one morning
in a New England hotel room to realise
all our acts of waking are indistinguishable.
Not the facts of linen and street noise
but our encounter with consciousness;
and the same with our common touch
on any of our planet-large abstractions:
not the one we trust but Trust;
not the beloved but Love;
shared, undivided
all one.

Spade Scar

Field craft: the bloody hack of earth.
Today significant of peat, a half-tonne,
the bog cut and water risen to replace it.
The dark meniscus is trod as he turns
ground to barrow, barrow to ground.

A sod lifted, sits fat on the spade:
the tar of grasses carameled by time.
Bare to the wind it sweats cold.
Water beetles onto the blade and oozing,
the sod slides into the barrow's brawn.
The soil's roots flattened,
its poor hessian exposed.

With a grudge the barrow goes.
Leaving a trench hip-deep to the digger
and peat to dry. Its tweedy crumble
still holding water, a little,
to hiss cloudy
when handed to the fire.

Corset

Two rooms overlap: a woman with a stick
framed in summer morning light.
The colours stretch, play, and when they touch
she stumbles: a child resting on a three-bar gate.
Now her conversation is mostly mantra,
syllables echo like the old clock:
my Aunt who named her corsets
Fredrick, Arthur,
she lists boys names of the *belle époque.*
Why do I grudge her cadence and pity: the fate
of a generation born to be spinsters?
With arms on the table to steady her weight,
she gasps, pinched by bones locked together:
a first lick of hellfire, or the firm hold
of a new dancing partner.

Cwtch

I come to this *cwtch* to escape,
inch close to the stairs so I can let it pass:
the steam-piston charge, each step a kick
to the wood, the drumbeat on the landing;
finished while the front door
still shivers in its frame.

This cupboard is like the entrance to a tunnel:
a ventilator jury-rigged from an old Hoover,
the single bare lightbulb. The hard slam,
three quick steps: that always catches me.
Three quick steps then the stop in the hall,
for minutes, before dawdling off.

In here I can smell the damp in the walls,
the rain and pollen of the day
the cavities were closed.
And the third announces itself: step, halt,
stamp, the sergeant of the guard
ready for inspection.

Machine Gun Killer

at nine was what I wanted to be:
behind the muzzle's flare, breathing the pepper exhaust,
transported on the recoil's shudder.

Toy that is almost the real thing:
half as heavy as I was then, its finger-bending mechanics,
as greasy as a bike spanner.

I had to lean, lever the blank cartridges in,
wedge it between my shoulder and chin.
I shook under its weight –

the trigger cut my skin;
it fired and knocked me flat, like a boy I knew
who tried to start his brother's scooter.

The next time I rode its spring,
squinting at the garden through the flash and smoke,
the metal hot to the touch. I reloaded,

heard the bullets ring,
saw the bricks chip, the greenhouse splinter;
let the gun keep firing.

Allen Ginsberg Returns to Llanthony

In 1967 Allen Ginsberg wrote the poem Wales Visitation
while staying near Llanthony in Monmouthshire.

Thirty years estranged from your mud lover,
your flood river – away via London and LSD.
Will you range further, or take refuge in part
of this lifetime.
World in mind, mind put into world,
a vale in the care of coupled hills.
Noah's valley, where the Euphrates ran,
and stygian water sat in narrow canals.
Does the wind part reeds in your beard,
the rain shed blood, do fallen leaves
spread putrefaction; or scream out:
fear blood, fear putrefaction;
to ewes with lambs on the sun fired grass.
Under the constellation of Ginsberg:
six stars departing, becoming strangers,
all affection gone in the vacuum.
Poor, with no words for their mud lover.
Are you an ocean over Albion, overwhelming
Tintern Abbey, bursting the Wye,
reaching out to Kyoto, San Francisco:
the restlessness of an unborn generation.
Or the sun bubbling on a pool of water,
that could be a spring plying
river curves into the earth;
that could be yellow light
making shadows play
on its cool lover.

The Ottomans

My Uncle is an Ottoman.
Sometimes I stay at his house,
its old walls keep out the city noise,
all you hear is the splash of water;
cool an hour and a half after noon.

He is a polite and generous man.
When the Ottomans had carriages
they would not raise their whips
but sat high up behind the horse,
and waited until it decided to go;

as the animal moved off they
would start to shout and thrash:
go left, turn right, go faster;
when it took them somewhere
they would give it a sugar lump.

I work in my Uncle's office,
he inhabits it like a clockwork bird:
his legs spring like levers, his coat
folds like wings; when he talks it is
as if a music box had opened.

I speak his language,
say *I* and *am* and *Ottoman*.
It is an old suit of clothes, stiff
at the collar and binds so tight
around the legs you cannot run;

it takes you round and round,
like the streets in the old town,
all leading to the Caliph's Palace.
My Uncle who sued for divorce
and found himself with two wives.

Materials (also Time)

City
(also epoch, modern):

Bilbao, the gaps in the limestone and water they call Bilbao.

Weather
(also epoch, ancient):

Last night's promised rain.

Railway Station
(also year):

Zumaia, that is the year of going to *Zumaia*.

Street
(also month):

Calle de Estazioko, Zumaia. The month I went.

Countryside
(also direction in time):

Last night's promised rain.

Seascape
(also speed through time):

From a ferry, through a barred and bolted porthole.

River
(also hope of controlling time):

La Ria, the salt water coming back from the sea.

Food
(also manner of divination):

Anchovies and eels, pressed against dry bread.

Drink
(also hold on time):

This morning's commuter carriage, sick with last night's cognac.

Machine
(also units of time):

Narrow gauge locomotive: gouged tunnels, slow turns, diving gradients; the repeating junk and waste ground.

Flower
(also person in time):

Call her Aurelia, the not-so-young ticket inspector, her courtesy and fraying cuffs.

Plastic Artwork
(also history):

The track plan of the Basque Railway Museum at *Zumaia*; the trunks and branches, steam packet and flying boat schedules of the world.

Animal
(also decade):

The manikins, unseen because they do not blink, dressed in berets, jerseys, a suit Ingrid Bergman might have worn; and abstract acrylic prints.

Sport
(also halt in time):

The Reds, *The Apotheosis of the Reds*.

Time of Life
(also end of time):

The cut lines and orphan platforms at *Zumaia*.

Music
(also reverse through time):

In Basque or Spanish, from Tannoys or transistor radios; strong or easy to repeat, that makes you want to sing along.

East

i.m. R.S. Thomas

In his imagination he was always walking out of the west,
as separate as one of his churchyard's stones,
following the path found and re-found.

A storm pressed by history into a man;
his intense noise, silence,
except a ray of sunlight pierce and re-pierce it

to speak to the bored present with the voice of a robin,
answer simplifications with the eye of a hawk,
to revel in nature seen and re-seen,

in words that have been mouthed by cliffs and beaches,
at the failures of grief and triumph of a birth,
words known and re-known.

Double

Chapter 14: The Use of Spies,
The Art of War, Sun Tzu

Two words come across, *Yin* and *Tao*,
to continue their lives in English.

What was already understood as *receptive*
or *female*, may now be *local* or *reward*;

quintessence or simply *the way*
may be written as *method of operation*.

The agent to be rewarded most highly
is one who serves both sides.

It is through double agents
other spies may be recruited, operated.

The general's ultimate defeat or victory
is in the *Tao* of *Yin* agents.

Windmills

These sons are something, out on the autumn promenade,
hollow eyes full of horizons, they should be something;
something suit, shirt, tie, they really are something;
it's time by their something watches. Fatter now,
their faces, something tans, simplify to silhouettes.

Finished late for the day, they'd leapfrog if they could,
invade the crazy golf course, stop it closing early.
One something on the green, one not, one indifferent.
One careful to choose a putter, the other handed his.
One chooses his obstacle, one starts from hole one.

They hoot as the policeman with the stop sign gobbles
the ball, nudge each other as it rebounds off a waiter,
are unbothered by the difficult windmill feature.
The score becomes a hoot in the dark, the winner
a something to debate in the many hotel bars.

At their high tide, all already somethings
and their sons surely will be somethings too.

Gunn

He had not thought death a handsome man:
bright eyes, sinuous, no longer young.
That Death would bid and he would come,
close, so close, still two, not one.
Old man, the black-and-white age has gone.
Poet, make your colours strong.

Death was secret like a tomb,
walled in shadows blind and dumb.
Death grew him in its stone womb,
grew him, monster, for its own.
Old man, do you hear bombers drone?
Poet, did your mother die alone?

That Death can shamble like a bum,
the one the pirates did not drown.
Whose plaintive eyes did they maroon?
That Death is cruel, and so much fun.
Old man, Molly will give you tongue.
Poet, write a rock and roll song.

Liege lord, where is your vessel from?
Captain, the tide is changing, it is dawn.

Eclipse

Wrecked and poor the sun reclaims
from moon shadow and night
a few sleepless humans
on a muddy tidal plane.
Ghoulish pilgrims,
their relics held on camera phones,
banal images, idylls of home.

Acolytes of remain and ruin:
the short pier and tall warehouse,
floors gone, windows put in,
cleared city blocks their refuges.
All that waits for rescue,
all that can only change,
to be made new and strange.

Again to the world's end,
watch it finish the same way,
they are the few you'll find,
where staked-out plots remain,
once so dear, graded by quality of view.
A landscape of heads looked out to sea,
as shadows withdrew from sand.

Sea and sand when gulls cease to talk,
settle under draining light,
together make a myth of dark,
the moon's black weight.
The sun gold for all infinity,
no time to alter, make it old;
no more light or matter.

A Life Included

From a father too deep to fathom, a boy called *Mud*.
Flesh to his brother's bone, wall to his friends' homes.
He was the island that made the river go to sea.

Was he was, all too soon: a pub, a glass, his eye.
A referee stepping in where no rules apply,
except it's an eye, always an eye they lose.

Wife to his scar's spite, husband to tender sight.
He took a trip across tropics: downstairs to sultry bars,
upstairs to mountains full of bears; where they fall, always.

A sweatless body tight as rope; an eye closed, peaceful,
in repose; a tattoo that made a mother lose hope:
Bugs in Nordic braids, horned helmet, ears flopped.

Made a father put cryptic work aside, something like:
sudoku, music, the mysteries locked in an ancient script.
Took an old fat video tape from a deep drawer,

sat cross-legged on the floor, sound turned down,
watched Elmer Fudd sing *hunting the wabbit, hunting
the wabbit*, to the melody from *Ride of The Valkyries*.

As he had before, his two sons, the three of them
rocking with laughter, rolling, turned to balls on the floor.

Talking with a Norseman

So, I'll say, it was *North* got me on track.
Sound the fool all the way to Byzantium.
Your navigators kept land in their sights,
happier, perhaps, with the rivers' many tongues
than the sea's pounding language.

Book, what the word-hoard
does not know, not well anyhow,
not much use in the fire's glow
or back to the storm
pulling on an oar.

Know, not know but is reminded,
as the tall trees along the roadside
show themselves again each autumn,
turning golden, dabbing the low sun.

Jove, shall we agree on that,
by Jove our common oath,
a name for something that's made up anyway,
still raining fire on his children.

Word, sound rune:
amulet for duration and re-birth,
charm against forgetting.
That little witch, what she had to bear.
They will pick her, her mica nipples,
from the bog, put her doll-like body
under museum glass.

Foot, measure of itself.
Boys again scout this parish, town–land,
then town, see the tribes holding sway there.
Know distances, know cover.

World, kaleidoscope of interiors:
cot and confessional,
schoolroom and lecture hall,
troubled youth and troubled times,
continuous war and continuing peace,
a low kitchen and the big sky.

Work, to know the back of your hand,
knuckle, finger and muscle.
So loyalty and homeland,
Christian and tradition,
every word, even alone, rings,
wrought white in the throat,
bitten, will rhyme.

The Entertainer

So I was chatting to this girl.
And I said I'm a professor.
Professor of what she said.
So I gave her my card.

So she gives me this look.
And I said, yes, professor of grief.
You teach grief she said.
So I did a little dance.

So she gives me this other look.
And I said I'm more of a song and dance man.
You're funny she said.
So I burst into tears, and so did she.

★

So I went to the doctor.
And I said my brother's died.
Why are you carrying a coconut he said.
So I introduced him.

So he gave me this look.
And I said can't you see the resemblance.
That's a split coconut he said.
So I became an autodidact.

So I went to the library.
And I said direct me to the grief section.
No food in the library she said.
So I took my brother to the park.

*

So they made me a professor.
And I said to my brother you're no coconut.
Gottle o'gear he said.
So I got him one.

Der Himmel über Berlin

The lofty half of an expletive,
partner to ground thumper *Gott*;
sounding like heaven or the angels.

Über misheard whisper:
Oberleutnant, Übermensch.
Sleepless searchlights

seek for pilots, supermen;
tire the eyes of grounded angels,
their blasted bodies, blasted eyes

filled with the sky over Berlin.
Their wounded shoulders
touched by the sky over Berlin.

They did not fly here,
will not fly from here
on wings of desire.

Der Himmel über Berlin is the German title of the
1987 film *Wings of Desire.*

Crimson–speckled

Asleep by the lamp left on overnight
are all the shades of winter imagination:
furry or naked, gawping or blind,
mouth-less and horned with antennae.

Moths left marooned in the dull morning,
so fine they could have been spun from banal dark,
copper dusk, lead morning; so fine
a careless thought might dissolve them.

And there is one discarded party dress:
white, dizzy with polka dots;
unfolding near the light, it vanishes
becoming crimson specks dancing in the eye.

The History of Cinema

Cast, blown and hammered,
with no obvious workings, Anubis
from an age of wax and steam.

Its tarnished mirrors duct light,
hallow lamp, bulbous lenses,
open a door in a whitewashed wall.

Familiar, out of reach, the image blisters
with diffident glare: a cave,
skeleton shadows, then whole bodies;

fields of eclipse flowers.
You can walk in, a dazzled ghost,
test your substance against the wall.

At first inanimate, its handle
is soon giddy with its own clockwork.
A wayward prayer wheel,

pulling the film blinking,
too fast, too slow,
the scenes somebody saved,

spliced together: monochrome,
hand coloured with greasepaint.
A winter sunrise, gaudy yellow windmill;

swans run on the river, lift in flight,
as pure white stick birds;
leave their grey silhouettes to float;

a viper strikes out from whips of grass.
Each long grass a viper, your hands a viper
if you make the shadows dart.

In the dusk there are cherry-red home fires:
a young mother, her boy
long, and climbing like a lynx.

The little hunter catches a finch,
holds it fluttering in his hand,
squeezing it too tight he smothers it.

Inconsolable, until his mother cups her hands,
sets a shadow flying, yellow, across the wall.

Making Love

I think that we were meant to...
Is it *treat* as if we were nations
or better *meet* as friends.
To have no buts
and simply wait 'til fate instructs.
Fate though never interrupts.
Oh: *sighs, eyes, easy, thighs.*
Oh: *find, kind, miss, bliss.*

In exquisite orbit on your...
Is it *rim*
or better *promise held within.*
Both pleasure and pain
in equal measure, at once the same.
With no words the meaning plain.
Oh: *insane, flame, be, flee.*
Oh: *quest, rest, crux, stuck.*

You are...
Is it *everything I lack*
or better *welcome heart and hurry back.*
Your soft magnetic air sublime,
wraps me in an ecstasy so kind.
That is I like your style.
Oh: *start, apart, qualm, charm.*
Oh: *light, flight, sun, undone.*

I fear you sense my...
Is it *following cloud*
or better *stubborn doubt.*
It is a flinching habit to say no
and pinch new love before it can grow.
Give no the elbow.
Oh: *aloud, shroud, spite, blight.*
Oh: *cruel, duel, bequeathed, heed.*

Banish fear with...
Is it *yes*
nothing better than *yes.*
Defeat strange love with a yes,
fate and doubt distress with a yes.
I would really like you to say yes.
Oh: *finesse, mistress, conquest, bless.*
Oh: *fair, dare, rare, flare.*

I watch your hair...
Is it *coil like a snake*
or better *hang at your nape.*
High on oblivion's plain,
a wordless freedom we will claim.
Enjoy the moment, don't explain.
Oh: *arms, charms, find, unconfined*
Oh: *sublime, entwine, sun, outdone.*
Oh: *me, thee, we.*

Acknowledgements

Thank you to the editors of the following publications in which these poems or versions of them have appeared: *Envoi, The Interpreter's House, Magma, The New Welsh Writer, Obsessed with Pipework, Poetry Wales, Smiths Knoll, Square Magazine* and *Times Literary Supplement*.

The poem *Masculine Happiness* was shortlisted for the 2008 Times Literary Supplement poetry competition.

I am grateful for the support of the Literature Wales Mentoring Service and Paul Henry in preparing this collection during 2013/14.

Special thanks to Amy Wack, Jamie Hill and everyone at Seren Books. Thanks to Judy Brown for her encouragement, and to the many people who have helped me along the way.

SEREN

Well chosen words

Seren is an independent publisher with a wide-ranging list which includes poetry, fiction, biography, art, translation, criticism and history. Many of our books and authors have been on longlists and shortlists for – or won – major literary prizes, among them the Costa Award, the Jerwood Fiction Uncovered Prize, the Man Booker, the Desmond Elliott Prize, The Writers' Guild Award, Forward Prize and TS Eliot Prize.

At the heart of our list is a good story told well or an idea or history presented interestingly or provocatively. We're international in authorship and readership though our roots are here in Wales (Seren means Star in Welsh), where we prove that writers from a small country with an intricate culture have a worldwide relevance.

Our aim is to publish work of the highest literary and artistic merit that also succeeds commercially in a competitive, fast changing environment. You can help us achieve this goal by reading more of our books – available from all good bookshops and increasingly as e-books. You can also buy them at 20% discount from our website, and get monthly updates about forthcoming titles, readings, launches and other news about Seren and the authors we publish.

www.serenbooks.com